MAGIC

JON DAY

With photographs by Zul Mukhida

Wayland

First published in 1994 by
Wayland (Publishers) Ltd
61 Western Road, Hove
East Sussex, BN3 1JD

Editors: Anna Girling and Sarah Doughty
Designer: Michael Leaman
Photostylist: Zoe Hargreaves
Adviser on photoshoot: Jon Day

British Library Cataloguing in Publication Data
Day, Jon
Magic
I. Title
793.8

ISBN 0 7502 1231 4

Typeset by Michael Leaman Design Partnership
Printed and bound in Italy by L.E.G.O. S.p.A

CONTENTS

AN INTRODUCTION TO MAGIC

We all know that there is no such thing as real magic. When you see a magician working at a birthday party or on television, you see someone who is using their hands and their head, very cleverly, to fool you. This is not meant to make you look foolish – just to fool you into thinking that something has happened that has probably not happened at all. In other words, the magician cheats!

I will show you how to cheat (in an honest way of course) so that you will be able to amuse and entertain your friends. I will also explain to you a little about the fascinating history of this wonderful pastime.

So jump on to my magic carpet! Hold on to your hat! You are about the enter the 'Amazing World of Magic'!

HOW TO BECOME A MAGICIAN

In order to become a good magician, you need to concentrate on two things. The first is **practice**. Practise each trick over and over again until you can almost do it with your eyes shut. Only then will you be ready to show the trick to your friends. Practise in front of a mirror so that you can see what other people will see.

The second thing you must learn is **presentation**. If you just go through the stages of a trick, in a mechanical way, your audience will find it quite boring. Presentation means dressing up the trick, with extra actions and words, so that it becomes 'magical', not just 'mechanical'.

There are several things you can do to improve your presentation. Try writing out the words that you are planning to say. They are as important as the trick itself.

You could use a tape recorder to record the words and keep playing them back until you have memorized them.

Sometimes you might like to dress up like a magician, with a cloak and a hat. A magic wand is also a useful thing to have. Make one out of a piece of wooden dowelling (you can buy this from a DIY shop). Paint it black in the middle and white at each end, using water-based paints such as poster paints or powder paints. To get a glossy result, mix the paints with watered-down PVA glue. If you cannot make a wand, an unsharpened pencil will do.

Remember that a magician is really just an actor pretending to be a magician. But your audience must believe that *you* think it is real magic. If *you* don't seem to believe it, you can't expect other people to believe it, can you?

THREE GOLDEN RULES

1 Check that you have got everything prepared *before* you start doing the trick. This means having *everything* ready and in the right place.

2 Never do the same trick twice. You may be asked to 'do it again'. This means that your trick has been successful and your audience wants another chance to catch you out – so don't fall for it!

3 Keep your secrets. If everyone knows how your tricks are done there is really no point in doing them anymore, is there? You can, of course, share your secrets with fellow magicians – but nobody else.

EGYPT: THE CUPS AND BALLS

Our magic carpet takes us first to Egypt. The year is 2500 BC.
The first *ever* known magician lived in Egypt at this time. He was called Dedi.
It is said that he could eat 500 loaves of bread and a shoulder of beef, and drink
100 jugs of beer, every day. He was very fat – and no wonder!
This is a version of one of his less fattening tricks!

What happens

Paper balls seem to pass through the bottoms of solid cups and appear beneath them. Then one of the balls disappears, and is found under another cup one metre away.

What you need

Three paper cups.
Four paper tissue balls about 3 cm across. Make them all the same size and colour.
A magic wand.

Preparation

The audience only sees three balls. No one ever knows about the fourth one. That is the secret! Stack the cups with one ball hidden in the middle cup. Lay out the other three balls in a row.

What you do

1 Pick up all three cups in one hand. Pull off the bottom cup with your other hand.

2 Turn it over very quickly and place it, mouth downwards, on the table.

Do the same with the next cup. Do this smoothly, and with the cup mouth turned slightly towards you. In this way, the hidden ball will not fall out or be seen.

3 Place the third cup down in the same way. Now put a paper ball on top of the middle cup. This is the one with the hidden ball beneath it.

Place a ball on top of it, cover with the other two cups, tap with the wand, then lift the cups to show that there are now *two* balls under the cups.

Put a ball on top of the left cup and cover it with the third cup. Tap with the wand.

4 Stack the other two cups on top of the middle cup and ball. Tap the stack with the magic wand.

5 Lift up all three cups together to show that the ball has 'magically' fallen through! You still have a ball secretly hidden in the middle cup.

6 Lay the three cups out again as before, but this time place the middle cup over the ball that has just 'appeared'.

7 Do it all again – this time placing the middle cup over the two balls. Tap with the wand and lift up the stack to show *three* balls.

8 Now pull off the bottom cup and place it down to your left. Pull off the next cup and place it down to your right.

9 Lift up the two cups to your left. Look amazed that the ball is not underneath them. Turn to look at the right cup. Tap it with the wand. Lift it up and show that the ball has somehow 'jumped across'!

GREECE: THE GREEK MARBLES

Our magic carpet now takes to ancient Greece. The ancient Greeks built wonderful houses out of a hard, shiny stone, called marble. A famous Greek magician was a beautiful woman called Circe. She could turn people into pigs – or so the story goes! She lived in a marble palace on an island.
Do you play games with small, glass marbles?
Find four that look alike and learn this trick. You will need a coin as well.

What happens

You appear to put just two marbles into your hand, but when you open your fist you are holding three marbles! Then, you put three marbles into you hand. You pull them out one at a time. But when you open your fist, you are also holding a coin that has 'magically' appeared!

Preparation

Note: If you are left-handed, read left for right and right for left throughout.
Put the coin in your right pocket. Lay out three marbles on the table. Hold the fourth marble hidden in your right hand.

What you do

1 Hold your left hand out, palm upwards. Pick up a marble with your right hand and place it on your left palm (you are still secretly holding another marble).

2 Pick up another marble and place it on your left hand with the other one. *At the same time,* drop in the hidden marble, too, and close your left hand into a fist. Your audience will think you are holding two marbles when in fact you are holding three.

3 Your right hand is now empty. Openly pick up the last marble from the table and put your hand in your pocket with it.

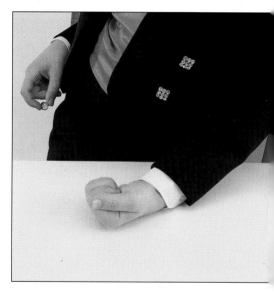

Then bring out your hand, with the marble once again hidden in it.

4 Ask: ' How many marbles have I got in my hand?' Answer: 'Two.'

Open your hand to show that you have *three* marbles.

6 Show that there are three marbles in your left hand again. Place them in a line on the table. Pick them up, one at a time, and place them into your left hand. As you drop in the third marble, secretly drop the coin in too, and close your hand into a fist.

7 With the finger and thumb of your right hand, reach into your left fist. Remove the marbles, one at a time, and put them into your pocket. Count them out loud as you do so: 'One, two, three.'

8 Keep your left fist closed. Ask: If I have put three marbles into my pocket, how many marbles are left in my hand?' You will get all sorts of answers. Prove them all wrong by slowly opening your left hand to show that you are holding a shiny coin instead.

5 Now do steps 1 and 2 again. When you reach step 3, put your hand into your pocket with the marble as before but, this time, leave the marble in your pocket and bring out the coin instead (hidden in your hand).

ITALY: THE QUICK ITALIAN COIN TRICK

The next stop on our magic carpet ride is Rome, the capital city of Italy.
In ancient times, over 2,000 years ago, Roman armies conquered much of
Europe. The Romans ruled many countries and introduced great new ideas, such
as building wonderful straight roads and warming houses with central heating.
Roman pottery and coins are still dug up all over Europe today.
This trick is called 'The Quick Italian Coin Trick'.

What happens
A small coin is dropped
down your sleeve and
'magically' plucked through
the cloth at your elbow!

What you need
Just one small coin (you can
borrow it from your
audience).

Preparation
First, learn this simple way to
make a coin 'vanish'.

1 Hold the coin between
your forefinger and thumb.

2 Force your finger and
thumb together with a
'snap'. The coin seems to
vanish.

In fact, the coin is lying flat
and is hidden from view by
the flesh of your finger and
thumb.

What you do

1 If you are right-handed, sit with your left arm bent. Rest your elbow on a table (if you prefer). If you are left-handed, bend your right arm.

2 'Snap vanish' the coin directly over your sleeve opening. It will look like you have dropped the coin down your sleeve.

3 Now pluck at the cloth at your elbow a few times. Then 'magically' produce the coin again!

BRITAIN: A ONE-WAY STREET

As our magic carpet touches down in Britain, we find a land steeped in magical history. Have you heard of the famous Merlin, who was magician to the court of King Arthur in the sixth century AD? Nobody knows if he really existed.

However, here are some magic facts about Britain that we know for certain:

- The first British magician we know about was a man called Brandon, who performed at the court of King Henry VIII in 1520.

- In 1814 John Henry Anderson was born. He became known as 'The Great Wizard of the North'. He was the first magician to produce a rabbit out of a hat!

- In 1100, a pack of playing cards was brought to Britain from abroad for the very first time.

- In 1571, a man was put in jail for performing card tricks. He was charged with witchcraft.

Try the card trick described here – 'A One-Way Street'. Don't worry – you won't be charged with witchcraft!

What happens
A friend or a member of your audience chooses a card from a pack of playing card and replaces it. You find it again, even though the person thoroughly shuffles the cards and you do not look at them.

What you need
A pack of playing cards with a *picture*, not a pattern, on the backs of the cards.

Preparation
Sort out the pack of cards so that all the back designs are facing the same way.

What you do

1 Carefully spread the pack of cards out in a line across a table.

2 Ask someone (let's call the person Sarah) to remove any card from the pack. Tell her to look at it and remember it. In case she forgets, tell her to show it to someone else. Warn them not to whisper what it is. Let's say it is the two of hearts.

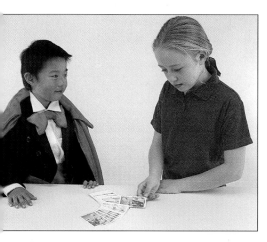

3 While she is doing this, sweep up the rest of the cards, from left to right, using your left hand.

4 Place the pack in your right hand. As you do so, twist the pack around so that the pictures on the backs of the cards are now upside down.

5 Ask Sarah to replace her card anywhere in the pack. As long as she has not turned her card upside down too, hers will now be the only one with its picture the opposite way round to the rest. If she *has* turned his card around, quickly turn the pack around once more before she returns her card. Just pass the pack from one hand to the other, turning the pack as you do so. This makes it look less obvious.

6 Ask Sarah to shuffle the pack of cards. Take the pack back. Spread the cards between your hands, looking for the edge of Sarah's card. It should stick out like a sore thumb!

7 When you see the card, just cut the pack to bring it to the top and place the pack down on the table. (Tap it with a magic wand if you like).

8 Ask Sarah to name her card.
She will answer: 'It was the two of hearts.'
You say: 'Please turn over the top card, Sarah.'
Watch her face when she realizes that it is her card.

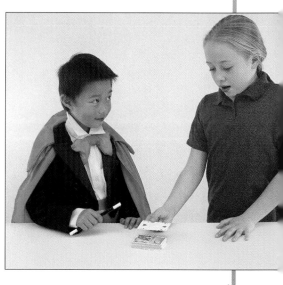

THE USA: THE GREAT ESCAPE

Leaving Europe behind us, now we fly supersonic on our magic carpet, faster than Concorde, across the Atlantic Ocean to the USA.
The first American magician we know about was Jacob Philadelphia.
He was born in 1735 – in Philadelphia. Strangely enough, he never performed in his own country. The most famous American magician, however, was Harry Houdini. Houdini was an escapologist. He could escape from anything and anywhere. No prison cell, no chains, no handcuffs, were strong enough to hold him.

This is a trick in honour of Harry Houdini.

What happens
A ring is tied on to a piece of string. Both ends of the string are held by a member of the audience. A handkerchief is thrown over both the ring and the string. You reach underneath and instantly bring out the ring. It has 'escaped' from the string!

What you need
A piece of string, about 1 m long.
A clean handkerchief.
A finger ring (you could borrow this from a member of your audience).

What you do
The secret of this trick is a special, false knot. You can tie it in front of your audience – but be careful not to let anyone watch too closely.

1 Fold the string in half and push the loop through the ring.

2 Then pull the loop back and over the ring.

3 Now pull both ends of the string tightly.

What you do

1 Ask someone (let's call her Marie) to hold both ends of the string.

2 Drape the handkerchief over the ring. Now place both your hands beneath the handkerchief. Ask Marie to bring her hands a little closer together (to give a little slack in the string).

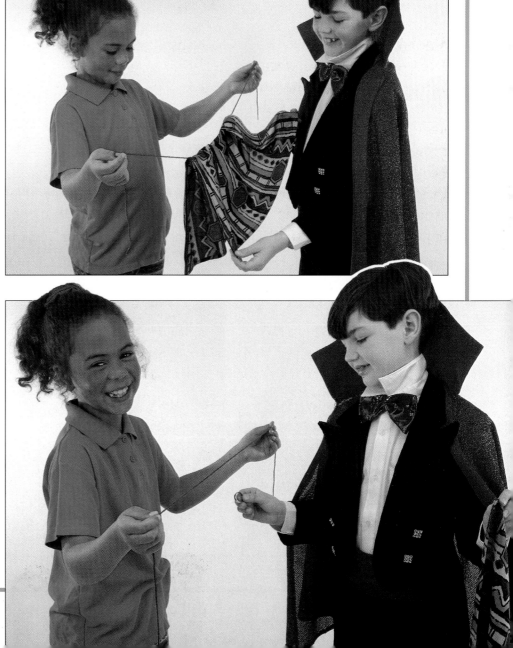

3 To remove the ring, just push the loop of string back up and over it. This action is hidden by the handkerchief and is possible because of the slack in the string.

4 Bring the ring out with a flourish and whip the handkerchief off at the same time. The person is left holding the string. Even the 'knot' has vanished!

15

INDIA; THE RIBBON TRICK

Now here we are in India. This is a land where magic
has been a part of everyday life for centuries.
One Indian trick in particular has amused and puzzled travellers from other parts
of the world more than any other. It is the famous 'Indian Rope Trick'.
It is always performed in the open air. The magician throws the end
of a long rope up into the air. It stays there!
Then a little boy climbs up to the top of the rope and . . . disappears.

Here is a rope trick for you to try – or rather a ribbon trick.

What happens

A length of ribbon is snipped in two – and then is 'magically' put back together again!

What you need

A piece of ribbon, about 1 m long.
A pair of scissors.
An envelope.

Preparation

1 Seal the envelope, then cut off a thin strip from each end, so that you have a paper tube.

2 Make a secret cut, about 3 cm long, across the envelope at the centre. Only cut through one layer of paper – do *not* cut right through the envelope.

Place the paper tube, ribbon and scissors on a table before you start.

What you do

1 Pick up the paper tube and open it up. Look through it at the audience to show that it is empty. Make sure your fingers cover the secret slit.

16

4 Pick up the scissors and start to cut the paper tube in half, upwards, across the centre till you reach the slit. Push the point of the scissors *underneath* the ribbon.

5 Then continue to cut the tube until it is in two pieces. Do not separate them – just hold everything together.

2 Hold the tube by one edge in your left hand (or right hand if you are left-handed). Pass one end of the ribbon through the tube.

3 If you bend the tube a little, you will be able to see the ribbon through your secret slit.

Now hold *everything* in your left hand (or right hand if you are left-handed).

6 Say the magic word: 'Abracadabra'. Then ask someone to pull one end of the ribbon. It is all in one piece!

CHINA: THE CHINESE HOOPS

Now we fly even further east, and our magic carpet lands in the country of China.
The Chinese people are very clever. In about AD 105, they invented paper.
And in the tenth century, they produced the first ever pack of playing cards.
If you ever get the chance to watch a Chinese magician, you are in for a real treat.

Here is a Chinese paper trick that you will have lots of fun with.

What happens

You give two people a large paper hoop and a pair of scissors each. You have a paper hoop and scissors too. All the hoops look identical.

Each person cuts right around the centre of his or her hoop. You end up with two separate hoops. One person ends up with two hoops that have somehow mysteriously linked together! The other person ends up with only one hoop – but it is twice the size of the one he or she started out with!

What you need

Lots of old newspapers.
Sticky tape.
Three pairs of scissors.

Preparation

1 Cut lots of strips of newspaper, about 10 cm wide. Join them together with sticky tape until you have three long strips, each about 3 m long.

2 To make the first hoop, join the two ends together with sticky tape. Make sure that you do not get any twists in the paper.

3 To make the second hoop, twist the paper strip *once* only before joining the ends together with sticky tape.

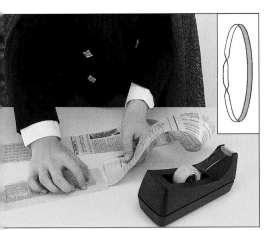

What you do

1 Make sure that *you* get the first hoop (you could put a secret mark on it so that you do not make a mistake).

2 Find two helpers. Give each of them a hoop and a pair of scissors.

3 Explain to your helpers that all three of you must cut right around your hoops. Tell them that it is a race to see who can do this the fastest. Tell them to take special care to keep in the middle of the strips of newspaper and not go off to one side with the scissors. Tell them to start after a count of three: 'One – two – three – go!'

4 From now on the trick works on its own. It does not matter who finishes cutting first. The surprise comes when one helper ends up with two hoops magically linked together! And the other helper finds that he or she has only *one* hoop, twice as long as the original!

4 To make the third hoop, twist the paper strip *twice* before you join the ends together.

JAPAN: THE MAGIC SWAN

Our magic carpet now takes a short hop to another eastern country: Japan. The Japanese are very good at making things. People all over the world use Japanese computers, drive Japanese cars and watch Japanese televisions. The Japanese also invented the amazing art of origami. This is a way of making models simply by folding pieces of paper. It is a very different type of magic! This is how you make a beautiful swan out of one piece of paper.

What you need

A square piece of paper. Swans are usually white or black – not pink! But use any colour you fancy. Make sure it is exactly square.

What you do

1 Fold the square in half diagonally and make a crease. Open it up again.

2 Fold both sides over into the centre like this.

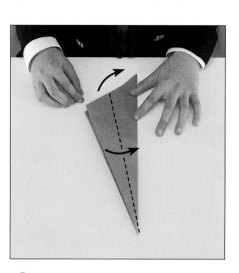

3 Fold the top half over along your original diagonal crease.

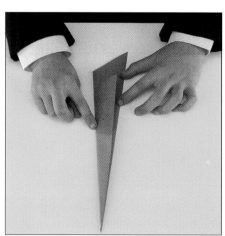

4 Now fold up both sides like this.

5 Open the model up, and turn it over.

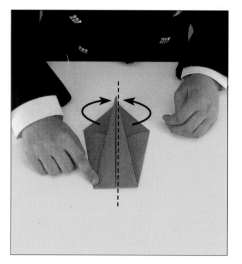

6 Fold the model in half so that the two points come together.

10 Fold down the back end and tuck it down inside the body. Then fold the end up again to make a sticking-up tail.

7 Fold in half down the centre line by dropping both sides.

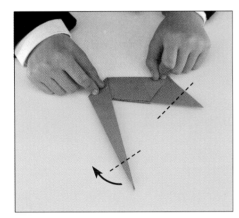

Key

A fold like this is called a valley fold and is shown by dashes.

A fold like this is called a mountain fold and is shown by dots and dashes.

8 Pull the neck up into a more upright position and re-crease the chest folds to secure it.

9 Fold down a section for the head like this. Then make two folds – back and then forward – to shape the head and beak.

FRANCE: THE MAGIC TREE

Off we go again on our magic carpet – this time to France.
In 1805, Jean-Eugene Robert-Houdin was born. When he was forty years old,
Robert-Houdin became interested in magic. And he found he was very good at it.
In fact, he was so good that he once stopped a riot by performing a magic trick!

Robert-Houdin was a great inventor of new tricks, which have been copied by many other people. He set out all the basic rules of magic that all magicians now follow. As a result, he became known as the 'father of modern magic'. The famous Harry Houdini even 'stole' his name – adding a little 'i' on the end for good luck!

Robert-Houdin's most famous trick was to magically create a fruit tree, which then produced oranges. It was surrounded by fluttering butterflies. This is how you can make a magic tree appear.

What happens
You produce a tree, 3 m high, from an old magazine!

What you need
An old magazine, the kind that is held together with staples. (Remove the staples before you start taking care not to hurt yourself.)
Sticky tape.
A pair of scissors.

What you do

1 Take one sheet of the magazine and roll it up into a tube.

2 Take a second sheet, and place it so that it overlaps the first sheet by about 5 cm. Continue rolling so that you now have a tube made from two sheets of paper.

3 Continue in this way until you have a tube of eight sheets of paper. Stop the tube from unrolling by fixing the final edge with sticky tape in about four places.

4 Stick the lower blade of the scissors into the centre of the tube and make a cut down of about 10 cm. Make six cuts in this way, evenly spaced around the tube. Fold out the strips all around.

5 Stick your fingers into the centre, then slowly and very carefully start to pull out the roll of paper. A tree will 'magically' appear!

6 You should be able to make a tree at least 3 m high!

GERMANY: THE VANISHING KEY

From France we fly across the border to next-door Germany. Probably the most famous German magician was Carl Herrmann. In the nineteenth century, he put on a show using practically no props at all (props are all the objects and equipment used on stage in plays, shows and films). He baffled the Tsar (emperor) of Russia, the Sultan of Turkey and President Abraham Lincoln of the USA. He even gave magic lessons to the Queen of Belgium. Carl was the son of a magician, Samuel Herrmann. His brother, Alexander, also became a famous magician and was known as 'Herrmann the Great'. And Alexander's wife, Adelaide, was also an excellent performer. What a magical family!

Here is a trick based on the magic of Herrmann the Great.

What happens
A front-door key completely vanishes!

What you need
A front-door key with a loop at the end. Ask if there is an old one at home that you can use.
A piece of elastic, 30 cm long.
A safety pin.
A jacket to wear.
A magic wand.

Preparation
Note: If you are left-handed, read left for right and right for left throughout.

1 Tie one end of the elastic to the key and the other end to the safety pin.

2 Fix the safety pin just inside the right sleeve of your jacket, at the top.

Hang the elastic down inside your sleeve. Adjust the length so that the key hangs just out of sight, about 2 cm up your sleeve.

2 Put the key into your left palm, still keeping hold of it with your right fingers. Close your left hand up into a fist. At the same time, let go your grip on the key. It will shoot back up your sleeve unseen.

3 Take your right hand away and casually show that it is empty. Do not make a big thing of doing this. Keep your left hand closed.

4 Tap your left fist with your magic wand. Slowly open your hand to show that the key has completely disappeared!

3 Just before you perform, secretly reach into your sleeve with your left hand and pull the key down into your right hand. Grasp it firmly between you forefinger and thumb. Your hand will hide the elastic.

What you do

1 Hold the key up so that you audience can see it. Hold your left hand out, palm upwards.

AUSTRALIA: YOU CAN'T FOOL ME!

Pausing only for refuelling, our magic carpet now takes us on the long journey from Europe to Australia. This is an enormous country, famous for its wild animals, such as kangaroos and duck-billed platypuses, which are not found anywhere else in the world. And you must know about boomerangs!
What do you call a boomerang that doesn't come back? A stick, of course!
The most famous Australian magician was Les Levante ('The Great Levante').
He died in 1978, at the age of 86, but his daughter Esme carried on his show.
Esme was an excellent magician herself.

I met The Great Levant many years ago. Here is a simple card trick he showed me.

What happens
Your friend or a member of the audience (let's call him Dean) chooses a card and puts it back in the pack. He cuts the cards over and over again. You turn your back and Dean starts turning the cards face up, calling out their names as he does so. (You can tell by his voice which one is his card, no matter how hard he tries to fool you!).

What you need
A pack of playing cards.

What you do

1 Give Dean the pack of cards. Ask him to shuffle, then put the cards face down on the table.

2 Reach over and lift off about half the pack of cards. Ask Dean to pick up the next card, look at it and remember it.

3 While he is doing this, slightly tilt the half of the pack that you are holding towards you, so that you can sneak a look at the bottom card. Remember this card. Let's say it is the two of hearts.

4 Tell Dean to replace his card. Put your cards back on top of the pile. The card that *you* have remembered is now on top of Dean's card.

5 Pick up all the cards and cut them. This means taking about half of the cards from the top and putting them to the bottom, in one block. Cut the cards again.

6 Now ask Dean to cut the cards as many times as he wishes. As long as they are complete cuts, and he does not drop any cards, the trick will still work. The two cards will still be together.

7 Now turn your back and ask Dean to start dealing the cards, face up on the table, calling out the name of each one as he goes. Tell him that you will be able to pick out his card, just by listening to his voice. All you have to do is listen for him to call out the two of hearts. The very next one will be *his* card.

CANADA: THE MULTIPLYING FINGERS

The final stop on our magical carpet ride brings us to Canada.
One of today's finest magicians is the Canadian Doug Henning. You may have seen some of his television shows. He has completely changed the way magic is performed. Instead of the traditional magician's outfit of top hat, cloak and bow tie, he wears colourful costumes using every colour in the rainbow.
He has introduced music, dancing and story-telling into his shows.

In fact, he has brought us into the *modern* world of magic. Nowadays, modern science and technology have brought us incredible new inventions, which almost seem to work by magic. We have cars, aeroplanes, cameras, telephones, televisions, videos, space travel, computers and solar-powered calculators.

Before we had pocket calculators, people used to do sums on their fingers. Did you know that you can multiply on your fingers? Try this . . .

1 Hold your hands out in front of you, with the fingers and thumbs spread out. Starting from the left, give each finger or thumb a number from one to ten.

2 To multiply by nine, you only have to fold down a finger to get the answer. For example, say you want to calculate 9 x 4. Fold down finger number 4.

3 Look at your hands. You have three fingers to the left of your folded-down finger, and six fingers to the right: 3 – 6. And 9 x 4 = 36!

4 What is 9 x 8? Fold down finger number 8. There are seven fingers to the left and two fingers to the right – so the answer is 72. Simple, isn't it? The bad news is . . . it only works for the nine-times table!

EVERYTHING VANISHES

Finally, here is a handy trick to keep up your sleeve.
Take the trouble to learn this simple series of moves and you will be able
to make any small object 'vanish'. Practise with a coin.

What you do

1 Hold the coin in your left hand like this, between your thumb and forefinger.

2 Bring your other hand forward to meet it. Make your right thumb go under the coin and your right fingers go over it.

3 Make as if to grab the coin, but as soon as it is hidden from the view of the audience by your right fingers, let the coin drop secretly into your left palm.

4 Continue the grabbing motion with your right hand, closing it into a fist and moving it away. Do not move your left hand, just hold the hidden coin with your second and third fingers.

Remember

This trick might seem incredibly simple, but please, please practise the combination of moves until it comes completely naturally to you. Try it in front of a mirror so that you can see how it looks from the audience's point of view. You must also put on an act. If you don't seem to believe that the coin is in your right hand, you cannot expect your audience to believe it, can you?

5 Now you can slowly open your right hand. The coin has vanished!

WHERE DO I GO FROM HERE?

I hope this book will whet your appetite and you will want to learn more about the wonderful world of magic. Here are some ideas.

Books to read

You will find many more magic books in your local library. Try to get hold of **Let's Make Magic** (Kingfisher, 1992) also written by me. It contains over forty tricks that you should be able to learn quite easily.

Other books include:
The Complete Book of Magic and Magic Tricks by C. Evans, R. Heddle and I. Keable-Elliott (Usborne, 1991)
Rainy Days – Magic Tricks by V. Bailey (Franklin Watts, 1990)

Magic clubs

Most large towns have a magic club where local magicians meet and swap ideas. It will be worth your while joining one of these clubs.

The International Brotherhood of Magicians has branches, or 'rings', in almost every country. Write to the world headquarters in St Louis, USA, for information about your local ring.

Here is the address:
The International
Brotherhood of Magicians
Headquarters
PO Box 192090
St Louis
MO 63119-9998
USA

The British Ring (No. 25) of the International Brotherhood of Magicians can be contacted by writing to:

Jeffrey Atkins
The Hon. Secretary
The British Ring I.B.M.
Kings Garn
Fritham Court
Fritham
Lyndhurst
Hampshire
SO43 7HH

Magic magazines

These will keep you up to date with the latest news and tricks. They also contain advertisements by manufacturers of magic equipment from all over the world. Write to the publishers to find out how to order copies.

Abracadabra (weekly)
Goodliffe Publications Ltd
150 New Road
Bromsgrove
Worcestershire
B20 2LG
UK

Genii (monthly)
PO Box 36068
Los Angeles
CA 90036
USA

Magic (monthly)
Stan Allen & Associates
7380 South Eastern Avenue
Suite 124-179
Las Vegas
NV 89123
USA

INDEX

The entries in **bold** indicate the magic tricks that are illustrated step by step.

With thanks to the pupils of Somerhill School, Hove, for their co-operation in the making of this book.